W9-CHL-235

One of a Kind

Program Authors

Connie Juel, Ph.D.

Jeanne R. Paratore, Ed.D.

Deborah Simmons, Ph.D.

Sharon Vaughn, Ph.D.

Copyright © 2011 by Pearson Education, Inc., or its affiliates. All Rights Reserved.
Printed in the United States of America. This publication is protected by copyright, and permission
should be obtained from the publisher prior to any prohibited reproduction, storage in a retrieval
system, or transmission in any form or by any means, electronic, mechanical, photocopying,
recording, or likewise. For information regarding permissions, write to Pearson Curriculum Group
Rights & Permissions, One Lake Street, Upper Saddle River, New Jersey 07458.

Pearson, Scott Foresman, and Pearson Scott Foresman are trademarks, in the U.S. and/or other
countries, of Pearson Education, Inc., or its affiliates.

PEARSON
Scott Foresman

Glenview, Illinois
Boston, Massachusetts
Chandler, Arizona
Upper Saddle River, New Jersey

ISBN-13: 978-0-328-45283-5
ISBN-10:   0-328-45283-1

8 9 10 V011 14 13
CC1

One of a Kind

Being Unique

Let's
Explore

Words 2 the Wise

We all have talents. But we all don't have the same talents. That's what **being unique** is all about! As you read this week's selections, think about what it means to be unique.

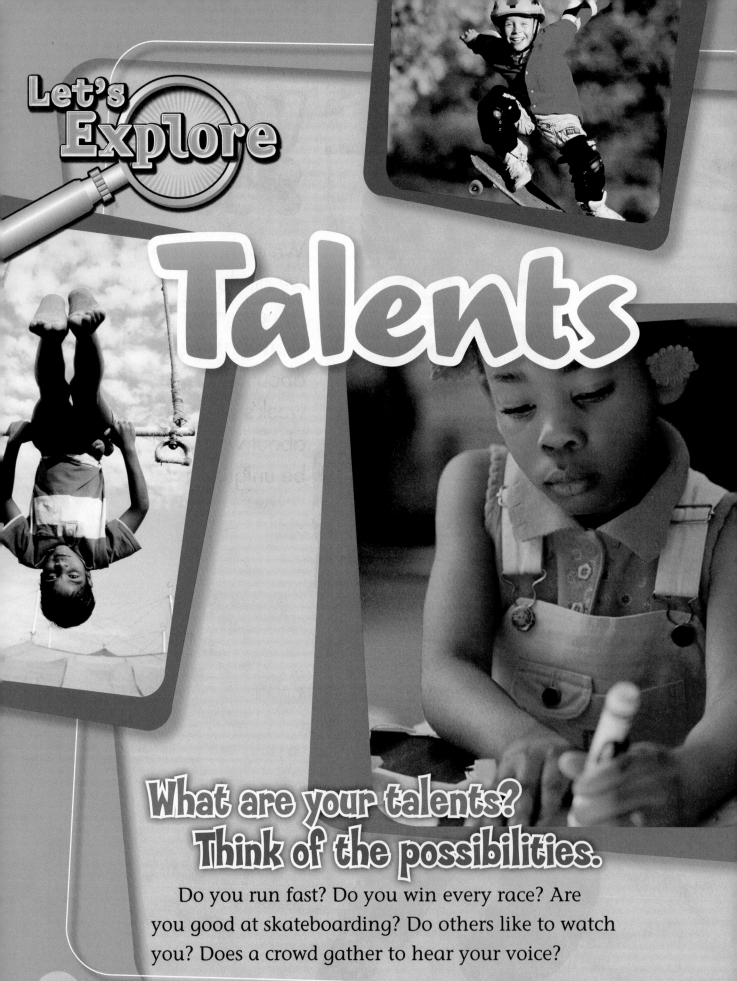

Let's Explore

Talents

What are your talents? Think of the possibilities.

Do you run fast? Do you win every race? Are you good at skateboarding? Do others like to watch you? Does a crowd gather to hear your voice?

Each person has a talent. Talents make us unique. A prodigy is a child who has lots of talent. Many people don't discover their talents until they are older.

Maybe you are not a fast runner. Maybe you do not want to join a singing group. That's fine. You might be better at making toys. You might be better at writing stories. Find out. All you have to do is try!

Very Young, Very Talented

by Phyllis J. Perry

Everyone has talent. Some people show great talent when they are very young.

An audience likes to watch talented children. The audience thinks children are amazing.

Some children in history have shown a unique talent early. Some showed a great talent when they were two years old!

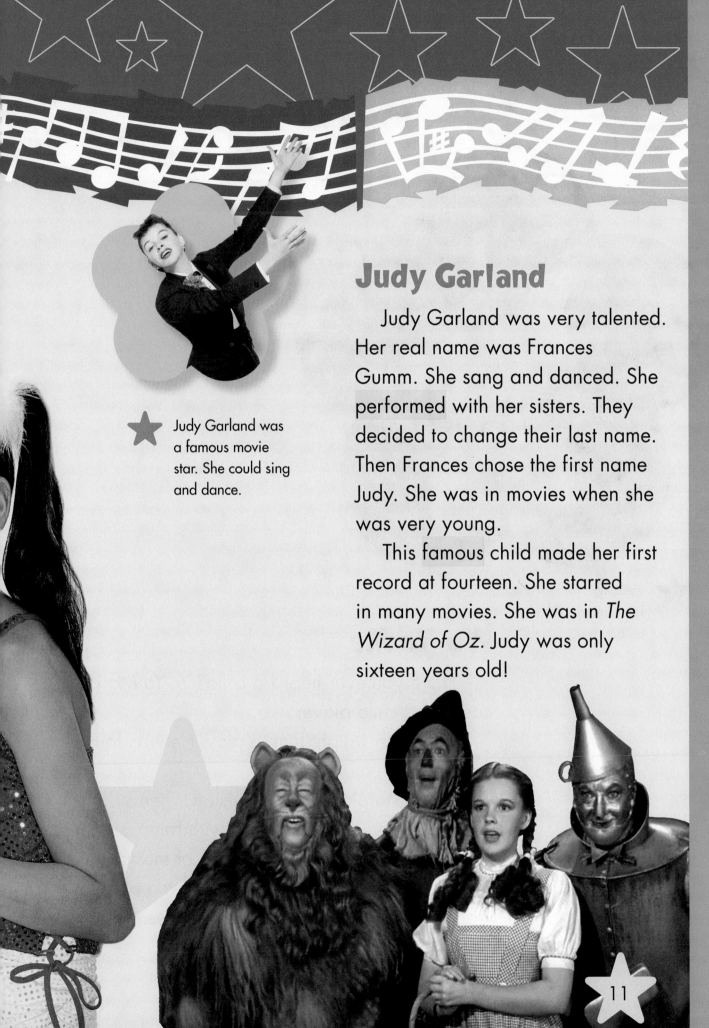

Judy Garland

Judy Garland was very talented. Her real name was Frances Gumm. She sang and danced. She performed with her sisters. They decided to change their last name. Then Frances chose the first name Judy. She was in movies when she was very young.

This famous child made her first record at fourteen. She starred in many movies. She was in *The Wizard of Oz*. Judy was only sixteen years old!

Judy Garland was a famous movie star. She could sing and dance.

★ Yo-Yo Ma
is a famous
cello player.

Yo~Yo Ma

Have you ever heard a cello? Yo-Yo Ma is a famous cello player.

His father taught him to play. He was four years old.

Yo-Yo Ma played on television when he was eight. He has played with famous orchestras. He plays many types of music. He plays jazz. He plays pop. He even plays rock! His music is also in many movies.

Tori Amos

Tori Amos is a piano player. She started playing at age two. She could play well when she was five.

Her skill is unusual. She does not read music. She plays by listening. She can hear a song once and play it perfectly.

Tori was invited to attend a famous music school. She was only six years old. Tori was the youngest student ever to go there.

★ Tori enjoys playing the piano for an audience.

13

Portrait of Wolfgang Amadeus Mozart, 1818, Barbara Krafft.

★ Some people think Mozart was the greatest of all musicians.

Wolfgang Amadeus Mozart

Wolfgang Amadeus Mozart was a famous musician. He began to play the piano early. He could barely reach the keys. He wrote music too. He was writing music when he was five years old. Mozart wrote music for the piano. He also wrote music for the violin.

Today music companies still print his music. It is still popular. Have you heard his music?

★ Mozart was interested in writing music when he was very young.

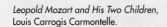

Leopold Mozart and His Two Children, Louis Carrogis Carmontelle.

Tiger Woods

Many children are good at sports. Tiger Woods started swinging golf clubs when he was one. His father taught him to play.

He won the U.S. Junior Amateur three times. He has won many championships since. He was voted Athlete of the Year when he was 21. Tiger is a very famous golfer. Have you seen him play?

★ Tiger is a winner!

★ Look at that swing!

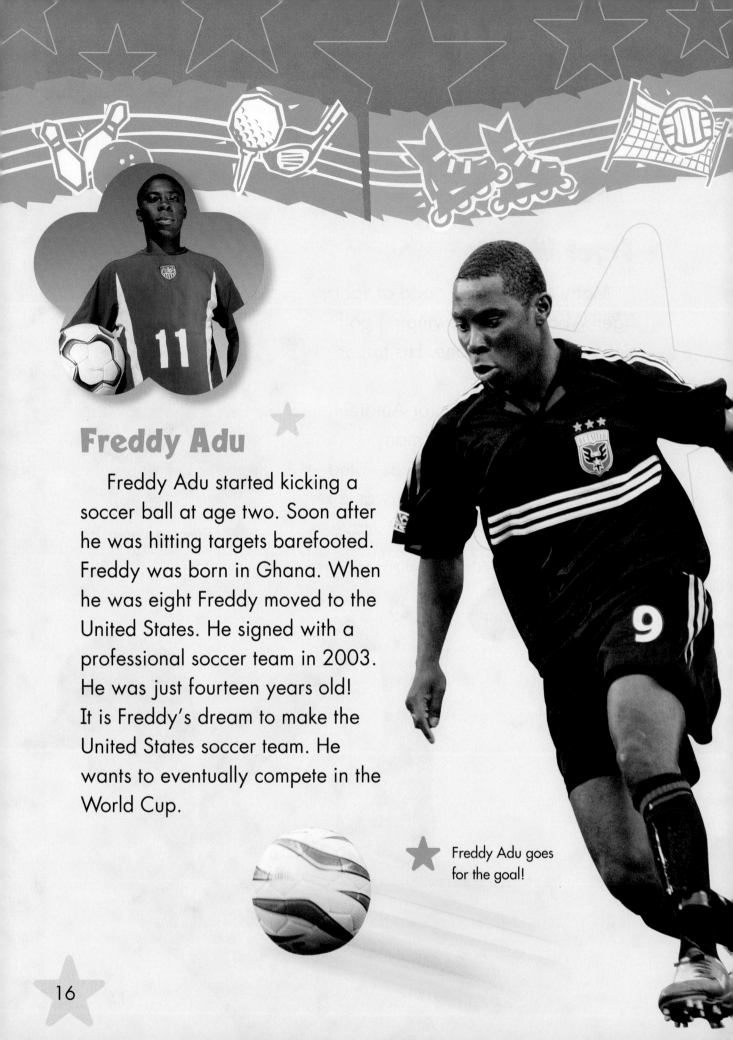

Freddy Adu

Freddy Adu started kicking a soccer ball at age two. Soon after he was hitting targets barefooted. Freddy was born in Ghana. When he was eight Freddy moved to the United States. He signed with a professional soccer team in 2003. He was just fourteen years old! It is Freddy's dream to make the United States soccer team. He wants to eventually compete in the World Cup.

Freddy Adu goes for the goal!

Pablo Picasso

Pablo Picasso was a famous artist. Picasso went to art school as a child. His father taught him drawing. He was ten years old. Picasso's paintings were amazing when he was thirteen. Today people all over the world know his work.

Woman with a Blue Hat, 1944, Pablo Picasso.

We all enjoy the special talents of others. Remember that you have unique talents too. Share your unique talent with others. Who knows? Maybe one day you'll be famous!

 Picasso's *Woman with a Blue Hat* is an example of his unique style of painting.

What Do You Think?
What steps can you take to find your unique talent?

THE TALENT

by Shawn Cambell   illustrated by Stacey Schuett

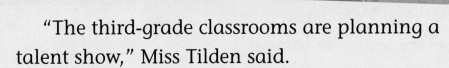

"The third-grade classrooms are planning a talent show," Miss Tilden said.

"What is a talent show?" Peter Cohen asked.

"A talent show gives people a chance to perform their unique talents. They do this in front of an audience. Students may perform a song or dance. They can also read a poem."

Peter heard the word *audience.* Yikes! His heart started beating faster.

"Your parents are all invited! It will be a lot of fun," said Miss Tilden.

I wonder if my parents will come, Peter thought. He began to feel nervous.

Peter thought about the show all morning. *What am I good at?* he asked himself. *I can play baseball. I am good at chess. But what else can I do?*

At lunch, Peter sat with his friends Ethan, Maria, and Jill. Ethan suddenly began to sing loudly. He was a good singer.

"Guess what I am doing for the talent show," he sang. The lunchroom kids started clapping. His friends smiled.

"You could recite one of your poems at the talent show," Jill told Maria.

"I could paint something," Jill said.

"What will you do, Peter?" asked Ethan.

"I don't know," Peter said. "I'm nervous in front of people. This is going to be hard."

"Maybe we could do something together," Ethan said.

"That would be cool!" said Jill.

"Let's meet at my house after school to plan," Peter said. "We can think of a way to show all of our talents together."

The group was sitting at Peter's kitchen table after school. They had no ideas. What could they all perform together?

Ethan came in wearing his favorite cowboy hat. "What's to eat?" he sang.

"Ethan! We don't have time to eat," cried Jill. "We need an idea by tomorrow."

"Wait! Ethan helped me think of an idea,"
said Maria. "Remember when we learned about
cowboys? Maybe we could be cowboys. We can all
sit around a campfire. We can perform something!
We can write a song."

"And we can all sing," Jill said.

Peter was quiet. He was listening to everyone's
ideas. Finally, he thought of an idea.

"I could play my guitar. You guys could sing,"
Peter said. He ran to get his guitar. His father had
played the same instrument when he was a boy.
He had given Peter his first guitar.

The friends worked hard. Maria wrote the words
to a cowboy song. Peter played the guitar. Ethan
helped everyone sing the words. Jill made a fake
campfire. She made vests for everyone.

On the day of the show, the group was ready to perform. Peter was nervous. He saw his parents in the audience. *I have to do my best,* he thought.

It was the group's turn. They walked on stage together. Peter began to play his father's old guitar. Peter looked up from the instrument. He saw his dad smiling. Peter wasn't so scared anymore. He felt even better when the audience clapped for him and his friends.

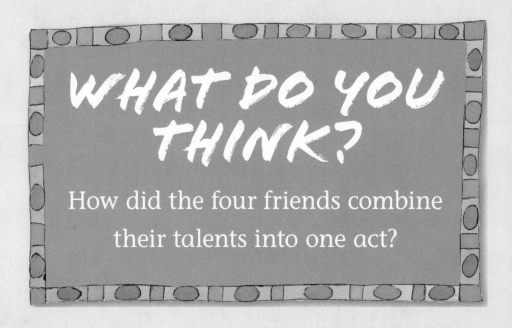

WHAT DO YOU THINK?

How did the four friends combine their talents into one act?

Weird and Wacky TALENTS

23"

Is your talent blowing giant bubbles with bubble gum? It takes practice. Lots of people enjoy chewing bubble gum. But only a few people can blow really big bubbles. People who can do this enter contests. Bubble makers use two or three pieces of gum. They blow slowly. The world's record for the biggest bubble is 23 inches!

▲ Try playing spoons at home!

Some people play piano. Others play violin. Some people play spoons! People who play spoons use serving spoons, soup spoons, or wooden spoons. A spoon player holds two spoons together. The handles go between the fingers. The thumb holds them in place. Spoon players keep the beat by tapping the spoons on their legs.

Paul Cinquevalli is the first famous juggler.

Juggling is not only a talent. It is also an art. There is a history of the world's greatest jugglers. The first famous juggler was born in Poland in 1859. He invented most of his tricks. He juggled balls, long sticks, hats, umbrellas, suitcases, and chairs!

Can you make weird faces? Is this your special talent? Do you make people laugh with the many faces you make? Some people can curl their tongues. Some can raise one eyebrow or wiggle their ears. Do you have a weird or wacky talent to share?

4 FOR 2 DO

Word Play

Cowboy is a compound word. It is made up of two smaller words, *cow* and *boy*. How many compound words can you think of? Write a list of five more compound words.

Making Connections

What talent do you have that you would share in a class talent show? How would you show your talent?

On Paper

Mozart played the piano. Yo-Yo Ma plays the cello. In the talent show, Peter plays the guitar. What is your favorite instrument? It could be one you can play or one you enjoy listening to others play. Describe it and explain why it's your favorite.

From TOP to Bottom

Contents

FROM TOP TO Bottom

Words 2 the Wise

Mountains and oceans are exciting places to explore. They **challenge** us! As you read, think about what you know about mountains and oceans.

Let's Explore

Mountains

Looking at mountains can fill us with wonder. But do you know how important they are for life on Earth?

Each continent
has mountains.

Mountains are beautiful. Just the
sight of them can affect your mood.
But mountains are more than a cool
sight. They are more than a boost to
your spirit. Many people live in the
mountains. About one in every ten
people lives there. We also get fresh
water from mountains.

Mountains often exist in oceans. Some islands are really mountains. They are the tops that show above water. The highest mountains in the world are in the Himalayas. Mount Everest is there. It has the highest peak on our planet. It has a height of more than 29,000 feet! Would you ever want to climb it?

Tallest Mountains on Each Continent

Asia
Mount Everest .... 29,035 ft.

South America
Aconcagua .... 22,831 ft.

North America
Mount McKinley .... 20,320 ft.

Africa
Mount Kilimanjaro ..... 19,563 ft.

Europe
Mount Elbrus .... 18,481 ft.

Australia/Oceania
Puncak Jaya .... 16,023 ft.

Antarctica
Vinson Massif .... 16,066 ft.

FROM TOP TO BOTTOM

Go Climb A Mountain

by Dave Brook

Climbing a mountain can be the most challenging thing you've ever done!

You want to learn more about mountain climbing. Imagine yourself breathing the fresh air. You can feel the cool wind on your face. Maybe one day you will climb a mountain. But you will need to learn many things before you climb.

First you need to prepare your body for a climb.

You can prepare your body with exercise. Running, hiking, and bicycling will help.

A climber gets ready to climb a mountain.

You should also practice being calm. A mountain climber's gear feels heavy. Climbers will get tired. They must stay calm. Otherwise, they will not reach the top.

The air on a mountain is very cold. Mountain climbers bring extra clothes. They layer them to stay warm.

gear things used for a climb, such as backpacks

Water is important to people who scale mountains. Climbers need to drink a lot of water. It keeps them from getting dizzy. Your body needs plenty of water.

There are other dangers. Climbers may have trouble breathing. There is less oxygen closer to the summit. The summit is the highest point. Careful climbers take a container of oxygen.

Climbers need water and oxygen.

It is also important to know the weather. Get good weather reports. Many storms can be dangerous. Climbers do not want to climb after a heavy snowfall! It takes lots of practice to know when to climb. Some famous climbers are still learning!

A climber climbs the ice on Mount Everest.

Peak Performers

Edmund Hillary and Tenzing Norgay didn't know if they could reach the peak of Mount Everest. Mount Everest is the highest point on Earth. But they wanted to try. Edmund Hillary is from New Zealand. Tenzing Norgay was from Nepal. They wanted to reach the top. Many people thought it was impossible. They reached it on May 29, 1953. They were the first humans to reach the peak.

Norgay and Hillary take a break while climbing Mount Everest in May 1953.

Both climbers were strong. They had learned from other climbs. It took them seven weeks to climb. It took them only three days to come down. Think of climbing stairs. It is hard to walk up. It is always easier to come down.

Peter Hillary is Edmund Hillary's son. He became a climber too. He stood on the summit of Mount Everest in 1990. He did it again in 2002. Maybe someday his children will try too.

Both Sir Edmund Hillary and his son, Peter, have climbed Mount Everest.

On May 10, 2005, Annabelle Bond, at age 36, smashed the women's record for climbing the highest peaks on the seven continents. She accomplished this feat in just 360 days.

Tom Whittaker also reached the summit of Mount Everest. He was the first person with a disability to do it. He thought he would never scale a mountain again. His knees were hurt in a car accident. But the accident didn't stop him. Whittaker tried three times. He succeeded in 1998. His story gives hope to a lot of people.

Annabelle Bond and Tom Whittaker both climbed Mount Everest.

Mountain climbing is not for everyone. You must learn all you can before trying. You must choose your goals. Know your limits. Practice. Some gyms have indoor climbing walls. There are no bugs or rock falls. There is no bad weather. But a gym is a great place to practice.

Remember, climbing mountains isn't easy. It takes lots of skill. It takes lots of practice. But it's worth the effort.

What do you think?

What goals have you reached? How did reaching them make you feel?

Get Over It!

by Jamie Kyle McGillian
Illustrated by Nicole Wong

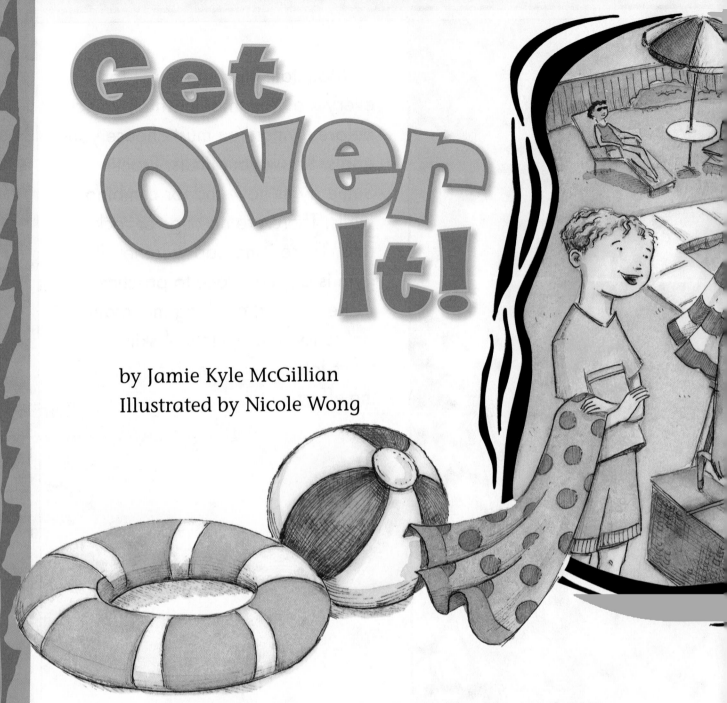

Has fear ever stopped you from doing something that could be fun? My name is Charlie. I overcame a fear that I didn't even know I had. It all happened last summer. My cousin Lisa came to visit. Lisa likes to try new things. She had just come back from mountain climbing. She was with her friend Finn. School was out. I had lots of free time.

Lisa, Finn, and I walked to the neighborhood swimming pool the morning after they arrived. I had never been there before. I usually go swimming at my friend's little pool. But the depth is only three feet.

There were so many people at the pool. I could hear swimmers jumping off a diving board. "Great! There's a diving board!" Lisa cried.

It didn't look too high from far away. Lisa
was a lifeguard. She said it was safe. I trusted
her. I walked closer to the diving board. Then my
hands started to get sweaty. My knees started to
shake. My stomach was upset.

"I'm sick!" I cried out loud.

"Maybe it's something you ate," Lisa said.
"Let's go home. We'll come back tomorrow."

I felt better when we walked away.

Lisa, Finn, and I walked to the swimming pool the next morning. It was a hot day. I couldn't wait to splash around in the cool water. But my heart started pounding fast as we got closer to the pool. I stopped walking. What was wrong with me?

Lisa and Finn looked at me. "Charlie, are you scared?" asked Finn.

"No, I'm fine," I said.

"It's okay, Charlie. You just have a fear of heights."

"Fear of heights? Why me?" I asked.

Lisa said that we all have fears. Some are more serious than others.

It was true. I never liked to climb too high in a tree. I never rode a roller coaster. And I always wanted to dive in a pool of cool water. Something always stopped me.

"Well, what can I do about it?"

"What do you want to do about it?" asked Finn.

"I'd like to get over it," I said.

"Good. Then we'll help you," said Lisa.

She took my hand. She walked me to the board. It was hard. I was fighting my nervous feelings. I wanted to let myself go. But I shut my eyes and stood in a frozen position.

Lisa told me to take long, deep breaths. She said that she would jump with me whenever I was ready.

I took two more deep breaths. Then I said, "I'm ready, Lisa. One, two, three . . ."

We jumped into the depths of the pool. The water felt so good!

"I did it!" I shouted.

Lisa and Finn were cheering for me.

I stepped up the ladder. I got into position with Lisa again.

That night Lisa, Finn, and I were making plans to visit a park. Maybe riding a roller coaster would be next.

What Do You Think?

What are some fears people might have? List them, and ask your family and friends if they know of any others.

FREE DIVING

More and more people are enjoying free diving.

There are beautiful sights to see in the ocean—fish, sharks, and colorful coral. Free divers get to see the ocean the way a fish would.

But free divers are not like fish. Free divers have to train to dive into the depths of an ocean.

Free diving is not an easy sport. Free divers must learn to take a deep breath and dive below the surface of the water without the help of a breathing machine.

● A diver swims toward the surface.

● A diver takes a deep breath.

54

Don't try this at home.

A diver needs to be in very good shape. He or she must prepare for the dive. For example, a diver must run or ride a bike for at least two hours daily. Divers spend about three hours a day practicing dives or swimming laps while holding their breath. Free divers work hard to have underwater adventures.

● **Divers swim together for safety.**

4 YOU 2 DO

Word Play

With a partner, write a list of five words from the letters in the words MOUNTAIN CLIMBER. Then compare your list to another pair's list. Add any new words to your list.

Making Connections

How is reaching the summit, or top, of the highest mountain the same or different from free diving in a large body of water? Give at least two examples for your answer.

On Paper

You're a sports reporter interviewing a mountain climber or professional free diver. What three questions would you ask?

Possible answers to Word Play: tan, man, brim, name, noun, mount, climb, limb, lime

Hobbies

Contents

Hobbies

Words 2 the Wise

Many of us have **hobbies.** You might like model trains. Your best friend might like to collect seashells. Someone else might like to make kites. As you read, think about this week's concept—hobbies.

Let's Explore HOBBIES

Are you looking for a hobby? You could collect things. Let us say you decide to become a collector. You can collect stamps. You could collect baseball cards. If you like the color blue, you can collect blue things. Do you have an interest in coins? You could start a coin collection. All you need to start are a few coins.

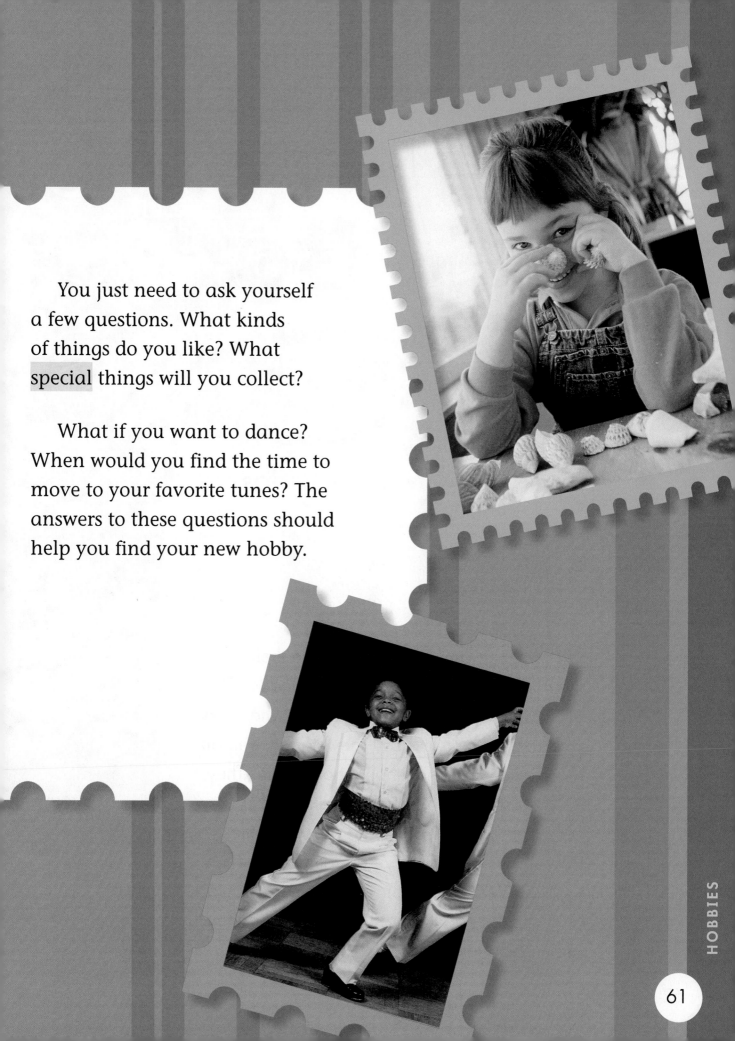

You just need to ask yourself a few questions. What kinds of things do you like? What special things will you collect?

What if you want to dance? When would you find the time to move to your favorite tunes? The answers to these questions should help you find your new hobby.

Glass Bottle Buildings

By Marcos Perlas

Bob and Dora Cain made their home in Treherne, Manitoba, in Canada. They were about seventy years old when they began their hobby. They started with an idea. Then they thought of a plan. They wanted to collect glass bottles. They knew they would need a lot of bottles. They spent three years collecting bottles.

What was their idea? Where would they keep all those bottles? Would their idea work?

Bob and Dora's idea was to build a house with glass bottles! Their friend Fred would help.

It would have only one room. They would build it on their land. It took two months. It was hard work but it was a delight. They had to be careful not to wreck the bottles. Sometimes the bottles would break. They finished the house in 1982.

Bob and Dora's finished house

What were they going to do with the house? Would they keep it empty? They used the house to show a special bottle collection. This collection had rare bottles. The collection also had bottles from other countries.

This was not the end of their plans. Bob and Dora had more bottles and more plans.

This is a picture of the church that Bob, Dora, and Fred built.

They decided to build a church. It took three months. This time they used five thousand glass bottles!

After they built the church, they put an organ inside. Then they added stained-glass windows. Then Bob found some old church pews, or benches. He cut the pews in half to fit them inside. The church was not just for show. There were at least three weddings at the bottle church.

Bob and Dora's wishing well had different designs and colors.

The buildings were becoming famous. Many people went to visit. Bob would give tours. They had as many as sixty visitors a day. They had more than seven thousand visitors one summer!

Even this was not the end of their plans. They continued to build. They made a wishing well. They used about five hundred bottles. They were all different colors. This made a rare design.

BUILDING	BOTTLES USED
House	4,000
Church	5,000
Wishing Well	500
Bathroom	1,000

Here are the number of bottles Bob and Dora used to build each building.

Bob and Dora had built three amazing buildings. But what else could they build? They decided they would build one last thing.

They built an outdoor bathroom. It was made with over one thousand bottles. Their son Joe helped with the plumbing. He put a sink in the bathroom. He also put a toilet in it. All their visitors thought it was great!

Bob and Dora spent about eight years on their hobby. They used over ten thousand glass bottles. It was hard work. But they enjoyed it.

Some people never show their collections. Other people share their collections. Bob and Dora Cain liked sharing theirs. Do you have a collection you'd like to share?

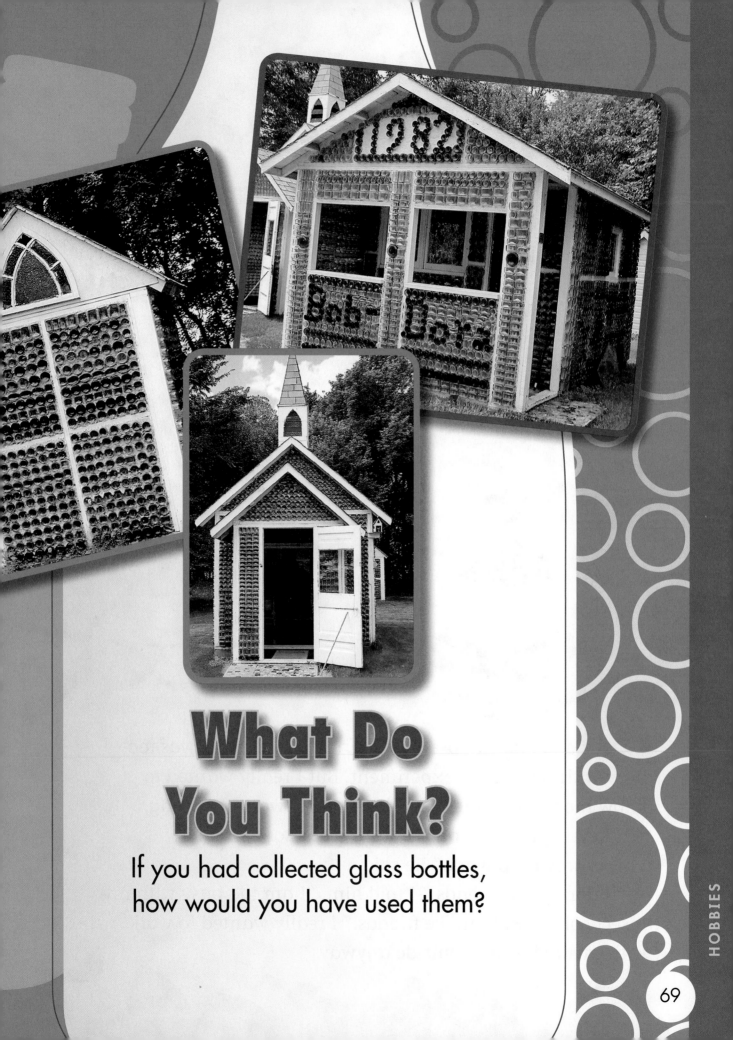

What Do You Think?

If you had collected glass bottles, how would you have used them?

WHAT ARE YOU LOOKING FOR?

by Sophie Caribacas • Illustrated by Julie Downing

My dad looked upset this morning. I think he was too busy with his science experiment. But I really wanted to know more about the insect his workers were observing.

"Kevin, please go outside and make some friends. This is grown-up work," he said.

"I don't need friends," I told him. "I am too busy with my insect collection to make friends." I really wanted to work with my dad. I went outside anyway.

That's when I heard a rustling near the bushes.
There was a girl looking for something in my backyard.

"Hey, what are you looking for?" I asked.

"A ring," she said.

I wasn't interested in rings. But she looked upset.
So I started to look with her.

"My name is Kevin," I said.

"My name is Tina," she said.

"I lost my ring. It is the best one I have in my collection.
I collect old jewelry."

I thought that was an unusual collection. But I didn't tell Tina what I thought.

The next day, Tina came over to my house. She wore a ring and earrings. She also had something around her neck.

"Hi, Kevin. I found my ring," she said.

"That's nice," I said.

I didn't have time for a new friend. I was looking for a special insect. I had been trying to find it for a while. I needed to show my dad my skills at finding insects.

"What are you looking for?" she asked.

"I'm looking for a very special insect."

"I can help you," Tina said.

"What do you know about insects?" I asked.

"Insects are good designs for pins and rings," Tina said.

I was NOT talking about jewelry. I was talking about insects. She didn't seem to have an interest in them.

"Look, I'm busy working on my collection," I told her.

"I know about collections. I know that collectors want to find out everything about their interests," she said. "I also know that insects have six legs. They can fly too."

Maybe I was wrong. She seemed to know a few things.

Tina came over the next day with her collection of old rings, necklaces, and earrings. There was a necklace with a special stone. It had an unusual shape.

"This looks like a beetle," I said.

"It is. The stone is shaped like a dung beetle. People in Egypt wore stones shaped like dung beetles. They were good luck," Tina said.

"The dung beetle! That's the insect I'm missing in my collection." I couldn't believe Tina knew about the dung beetle.

There were only a few places Tina and I could look for this dung beetle. There are thousands of kinds of dung beetles in the world. I was looking for the one that feeds on mushrooms and old leaves.

"I am going to look at the leaves on the ground," said Tina.

We both looked. It didn't take long. We found a dung beetle! What a delight! It curled up into a ball when we tried to put it in a jar. We ran back to my house.

"Dad! Look what I finally found!" I proudly showed my dung beetle to him.

"And all it took was a little help from a friend."

WHAT DO YOU THINK?

Do you think Kevin still thinks he doesn't need friends?

HOBBY HUNTING

Are you looking for a hobby but don't know how to start? Answer these questions to help you think of some choices.

1. What are some things that you like?

2. Do you like to collect things?
   - stamps
   - stickers
   - comic books
   - rocks
   - coins
   - baseball cards
   - seashells
   - fossils
   - other

3. Do you like activities? What kinds?
   - acting
   - building things/making things
   - doing puzzles
   - drawing or painting
   - playing sports
   - reading
   - working or playing on computers
   - writing
   - other

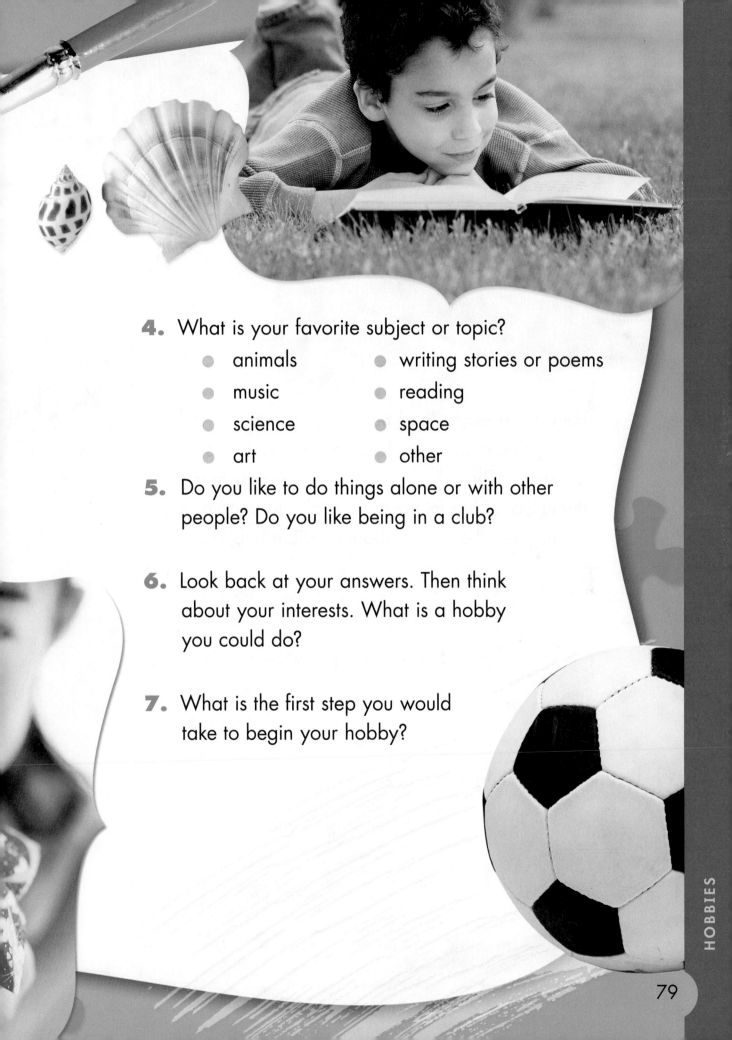

4. What is your favorite subject or topic?

- animals
- music
- science
- art
- writing stories or poems
- reading
- space
- other

5. Do you like to do things alone or with other people? Do you like being in a club?

6. Look back at your answers. Then think about your interests. What is a hobby you could do?

7. What is the first step you would take to begin your hobby?

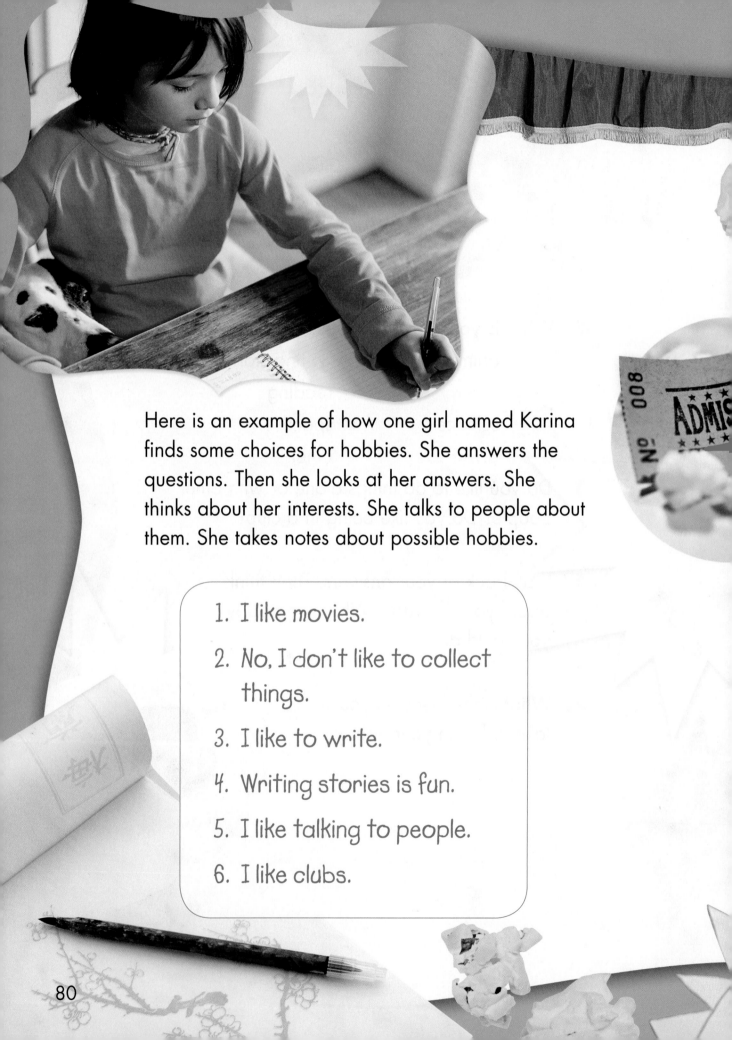

Here is an example of how one girl named Karina finds some choices for hobbies. She answers the questions. Then she looks at her answers. She thinks about her interests. She talks to people about them. She takes notes about possible hobbies.

1. I like movies.

2. No, I don't like to collect things.

3. I like to write.

4. Writing stories is fun.

5. I like talking to people.

6. I like clubs.

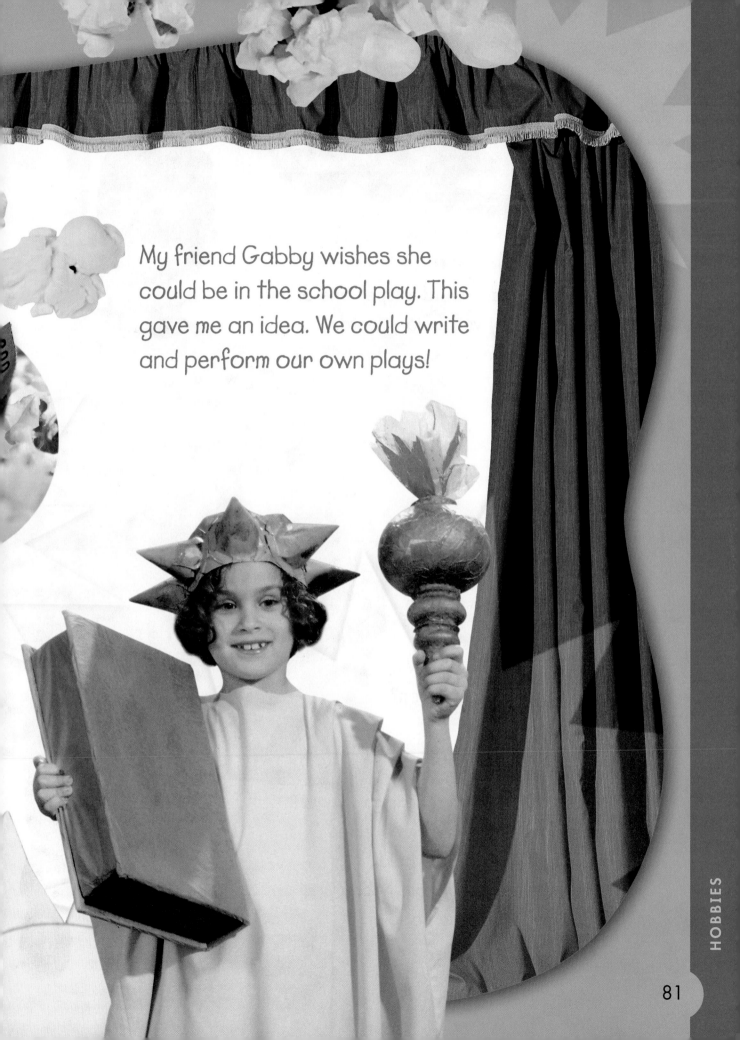

My friend Gabby wishes she could be in the school play. This gave me an idea. We could write and perform our own plays!

Word Play

Unscramble each word to spell one of this week's concept vocabulary words.

i c a l e p s

t i l d e h g

s e t e t n i r

s a l u n u u

l e c t l i o n c o

r e r a

Making Connections

What do Bob, Dora, Kevin, and Tina have in common?

On Paper

Bob and Dora made buildings using glass bottles. Kevin collected bugs, and Tina collected old jewelry. Write about your hobby or another interesting hobby.

Answers to Word Play: special, delight, interest, unusual, collection, rare

Contents

BEING THE FIRST

Let's Explore

Words 2 the Wise

Why do people want to be the first to do something? As you read, think about what **being the first** means to you.

Famous Firsts

What does it mean to be first?
What would you like to be the first to do?

Orville and Wilbur Wright built the first successful airplane.

Once upon a time, two brothers stood on a hill and dreamed that people could fly like birds. They were the Wright brothers. They built and flew the first airplane. It was an adventure. But they took a risk to even try. Now airplanes are a part of everyday life.

Neil Armstrong was the first person to walk on the moon.

George Washington was the first President of the United States.

Sandra Day O'Connor was the first woman on the Supreme Court.

Who are the people that do things for the first time? They are dreamers. They believe anything is possible. They are hard workers. They do not give up. They are role models for us. Look at what happens when someone dreams. We learn that we can change the world.

If you could be the first to do something, what would it be?

Over Niagara Falls

by Brian Shah

People love to visit Niagara Falls. It is a very famous spot. Why do people come? They like to look at the giant waterfall. The sound of the rushing water says, "Adventure!" There is no other place just like it.

For some people, looking and listening is not enough. These people are very brave. They like to do remarkable things. They want to be famous. They want to go *over* the Falls. But this is *very* dangerous!

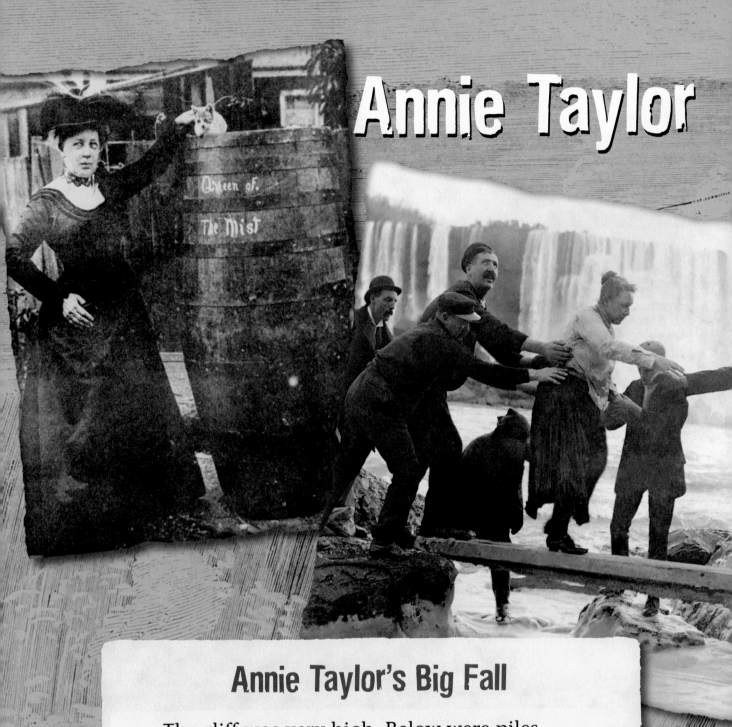

Annie Taylor

Annie Taylor's Big Fall

The cliff was very high. Below were piles of rocks. A great river flowed over the cliff. A wooden barrel floated close to the edge. The barrel was going to fall. A woman was inside! What would happen to her?

The year was 1901. The woman's name was Annie Taylor. She was a teacher. She wanted to be famous. She wanted to be the first person to go over Niagara Falls in a barrel.

The flowing river carried Annie over the edge. Annie fell and hit the water below. But she was okay! She survived this daring adventure. And she was famous!

Jean François Gravelet

The Great Blondin

Have you ever seen someone walk on a tightrope? It is not easy. Every step is important.

Jean François Gravelet (Zhahn Fran•SWAH Grah•vah•LAY) called himself "The Great Blondin." In 1859 he did something amazing. He was the first person to walk on a tightrope over Niagara Falls.

Gravelet crossed the Falls many times. He made the trip more exciting each time. He crossed at night. He crossed on a bicycle. He crossed carrying another man on his back!

Maria Spelterini

Maria's Crossing

Other people wanted to be like The Great Blondin. In 1876 Maria Spelterini (spel•ter•EE•nee) became the first woman to cross Niagara Falls on a tightrope. She put one basket on each foot. She covered her eyes. She did this for the people watching. She wanted them to say, "What a remarkable woman!"

Maria *was* remarkable. She was brave and fearless. She was one of very few people who had the courage to walk over Niagara Falls.

Jean Lussier

Jean Lussier's Rubber Ball

Many other people wanted to go over Niagara Falls too. But it was a dangerous and careless thing to do! Some died. People tried different things to make the trip safe.

In 1928 Jean Lussier (loo-SYA) made a special rubber ball. The ball was six feet high. It was very strong. Jean got inside the ball. The ball went over the giant waterfall. An hour later Jean appeared on shore. He was fine, thanks to his rubber ball!

The Miracle at Niagara

In 1960 something remarkable happened. Roger Woodward was in a boat above the waterfall. He was seven years old. The boat tipped over. Roger fell over the falls! He survived! People saw his orange life jacket. They pulled him into their boat. People thought it was impossible! They called it "The Miracle at Niagara."

Every year thousands of people from all over the world visit the Falls. Most are happy just to take pictures or go on a boat ride. But for a few, Niagara will always be a call to adventure.

1859
The Great Blondin, first tightrope walk

1876
Maria Spelterini, first woman tightrope walk

1901
Annie Taylor, first person to go over in barrel

1928
Jean Lussier in his rubber ball

1960
Roger Woodward, Miracle at Niagara

What Do You Think?

Which Niagara daredevil was the bravest? Why?

A Smoothie Sensation

by Rachel Mann
illustrated by Cathi Mingus

Hannah put a penny on top. The stack was very tall. It looked endless. "Good job!" said her friend Beth.

"How many pennies is that?" asked Hannah.
"That makes forty-two," said Beth.
"Only forty-two!" said Hannah. "That's not enough! I want to beat the world record. That's three hundred coins!"

"Keep trying! It's not hopeless," said Beth.

Hannah made another attempt. She carefully added more. "Number fifty-nine," she said. "Number sixty." The stack swayed. Then they fell.

"Oh, no!" said Hannah. Crash! The pennies scattered on the floor.

Hannah loved to read the *World Record Book*. She read about the long-distance runners and the smartest people. She read about people who can do impossible things no one else can.

Hannah attempted to break records. She walked a short distance with a milk bottle on her head. She did it for ten minutes. But it was pointless. The record holder did it for a whole day!

"Coin stacking is too hard," she said to Beth. "What else can I try?"

Beth looked at the book. "Drink a bottle of ketchup in thirty seconds!"

"Yuck!" said Hannah. "They can keep that record!"

"Blow the world's biggest bubble," said Beth.

"I don't like to chew gum," said Hannah.

"Someone baked the world's biggest pie," said Beth. "It was bigger than your yard!"

"Amazing," said Hannah. "But I can't bake. I need to find something that I am good at! Let's take a break."

"I'll make yogurt smoothies," said Hannah.

"Oh, good," said Beth.

Hannah mixed up the drinks. "I have an idea," she said. "Let's make the world's biggest smoothie!"

"That is a great idea," said Beth. "But how?"

"We have yogurt and milk," said Hannah. "And we can pick berries in the yard. But where will we mix it?"

"Can we mix it in the bathtub?" asked Beth.

"That would be a big smoothie," said Hannah. "But not big enough! We want to set a world record. We need to do something that no one has ever done before. I know. We'll use the public swimming pool!"

"I don't think they'll close the pool for our world record project," said Beth.

"You're right. Let's go to the neighbors' houses. We'll ask to borrow their kiddie pools. Almost every house around here has one!" said Hannah.

"Great idea," said Beth.

There was lots to do. The neighbors were excited. They helped collect the pools. They picked berries in the yard. They filled their buckets.

MILK

They poured milk and yogurt into the pools. They dumped in berries. They mixed it up.

Together the town made the world's biggest smoothie. It was great! Everyone had a cup. There was plenty for all!

Hannah and Beth were proud of their idea. Hannah took a picture of the smoothie. She sent it to the *World Record Book*. Hannah's neighbors helped her become a world-record holder at last!

What Do You Think?

How is Hannah's smoothie idea different from the other things she tried to do to set a world record?

GUINNESS BOOK OF WORLD RECORDS

Do you have a wacky talent? Can you do something that no one else can do? Maybe you could be in the *Guinness Book of World Records!*

This famous book tells about all kinds of unusual people and things. These are not everyday stories. Guinness World Record holders do remarkable things! Here are a few examples of what you might find in the book.

The smallest dog in the world is only 5 inches tall and weighs less than 2 pounds.

Imagine a dog the size of an apple!

5" tall

Robert Pershing Wadlow was the tallest man in history. He was almost nine feet tall!

You would have needed a ladder to talk to Robert Pershing Wadlow.

9' tall

8

7

6

5

4

3

2

1

Tony Hawk spins through the air.

2.1/2 times

Tony Hawk is one of the most famous skateboarders of all time. In 1999 Hawk raced off the ramp and into history. He spun in the air two and a half times. It was an amazing trick!

8.1 feet across

Don't eat it all in one bite!

Who doesn't love big cookies? In 1996 a company in New Zealand made the biggest chocolate chip cookie ever. It was over eighty-one feet across!

From silliest to largest to dangerous, the *Guinness Book of World Records* tells it all.

4 you 2 Do

Word Play

Use this week's concept words to make a sign announcing a new world record.

Making Connections

How are Hannah and Annie Taylor alike? How are they different?

On Paper

Imagine that you could set any world record. What would it be and how would you do it?

People and Animals

Contents

People and Animals

Let's Explore

110

Words 2 the Wise

People and animals can become good friends. As you read, think about what you know about friendships between people and animals.

Having a New Pet

Getting a new pet is fun. But it's also hard work. The pet needs to adjust to a new home. It needs to learn what it can and cannot do.

Families must work together. They need to communicate. Everyone should help. Each person should have a job. Everyone should help the pet be healthy and happy in its new home.

A pet owner shows that her pet is close to her heart.

It is important to realize that pets need special care to stay healthy.

You will need to spend time caring for your pet. Some pets need exercise. You may have to walk your pet or play with it outside. Do you sleep late on the weekends? Your pet may not let you. And remember that your pet will need fresh water and food each day.

PEOPLE AND ANIMALS

113

What if you go on vacation? What will you do with your pet? You could leave the pet in a kennel. You could also ask a neighbor to care for it. Or you can go somewhere your pet can go too.

Your pet's health is important. You must take your pet to the vet. The vet will make sure your pet is healthy.

It is important to take good care of your pet. A pet will change your life. It will bring you lots of happiness.

Making Friends with Gorillas

by Mark Rafenstein

Dian Fossey did more than study gorillas. She became friends with them!

You are in Africa walking along a mountain path. The forest around you is thick. Suddenly something big jumps out of the trees. A large, adult gorilla is standing in front of you! You are surprised. But so is the gorilla. He shows his teeth. You hold your breath. He makes loud sounds. He starts hitting his big chest with his large hands. You realize you might be in trouble. What do you do?

Most people would not know what to do. But Dian Fossey did. She was in Africa in the 1960s. She came face to face with a group of gorillas. They charged, or ran, towards her. Then they yelled and screamed.

Dian stayed calm. She sat on the ground. She turned her back to them. She knew the animals were peaceful. They did not want to hurt her. She realized they were protecting their young. The animals left.

This first meeting with the gorillas of the Virunga (vee-ROON-gah) Volcano Mountains would be one of many. Dian was a scientist. It was her job to study the mountain gorillas. Not much was known about this type of gorilla at the time. Fossey needed to get close to the animals to discover how they act. But they might misunderstand her actions. How could she get close without making them run off?

Dian Fossey studies a family of gorillas.

Dian Fossey knew that she could not just walk up to them. She would need a plan. She would first need to watch the animals from far away.

Dian watched a family of gorillas for many days. She did not distract them. She watched them look for food and play together. She learned a lot. She learned that this type of gorilla spends a lot of time looking for food and eating. Dian learned that they eat plants. Sometimes they eat ants and worms.

Dian Fossey studied gorillas in Africa. The areas in green are where she learned about their habits.

Mountain Gorilla Conservation Areas

Uganda

Area of Map

Kayonza

Buhoma

Bwindi Impenetrable Forest National Park

Ruhizha

Democratic Republic of Congo

Lake Mutanda

Lake Mulehe

Lake Bunyonyi

Kisoro

Virunga Conservation Area

Rwanda

Karisoke Research Center

Ruhengeri

Legend

National Park Boundary

International Boundary

0   5   10km

120

Dian also learned that gorillas communicate with each other. They do this by making different sounds. They also do this by moving their hands and bodies in certain ways. Sometimes they use their faces to communicate. When a gorilla shows its teeth it means, "Stay away. I am angry."

Dian had the opportunity to get closer to the gorillas. She learned to mimic, or "talk" and act like them. She learned to mimic a noise that gorillas make when they are happy. The sound made them less afraid of her.

Several months went by. She got within thirty feet of them. After two and a half years, a young gorilla named Peanuts touched her. She was thrilled! This touch was the start of a friendship.

Fossey became the gorillas' friend. One day Dian was feeling displeased about something. One of the gorillas saw her. He must have known she was sad. He came over to her. He spread his arm around her shoulders. He patted her on the head.

What Do You Think?

In what ways did the gorillas show that they trusted Dian?

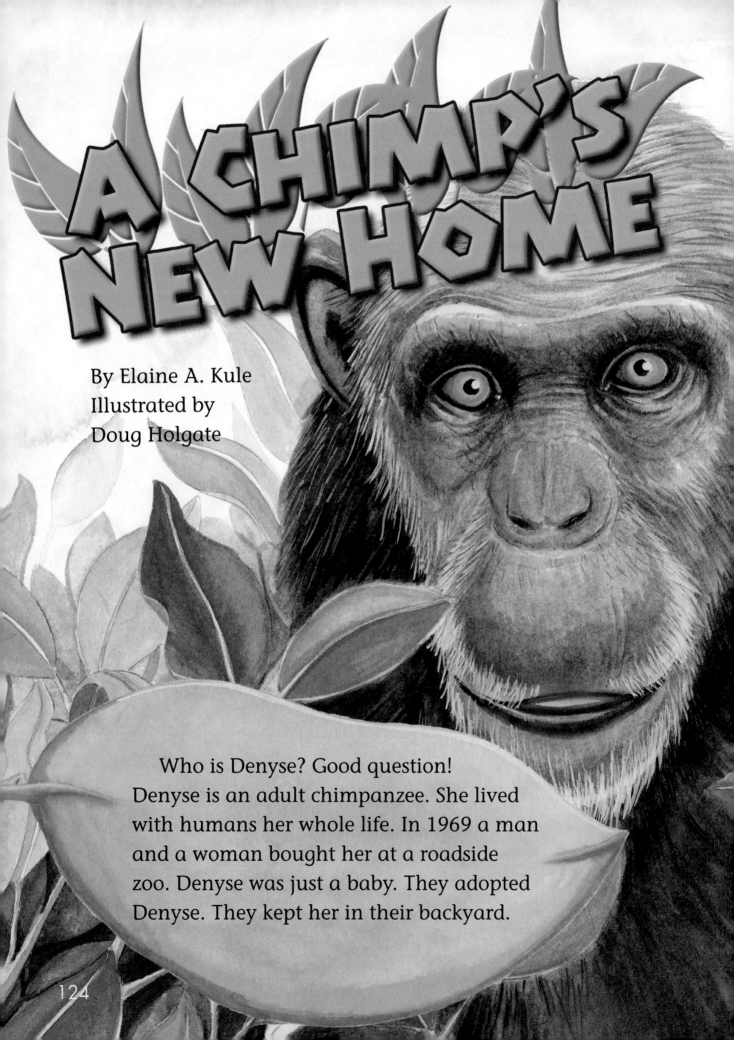

A CHIMP'S NEW HOME

By Elaine A. Kule
Illustrated by
Doug Holgate

Who is Denyse? Good question!
Denyse is an adult chimpanzee. She lived
with humans her whole life. In 1969 a man
and a woman bought her at a roadside
zoo. Denyse was just a baby. They adopted
Denyse. They kept her in their backyard.

The couple loved Denyse. They became her human "parents." She never saw another chimp while she was growing up.

Denyse ate chimpanzee food. She also ate human food. Some of her favorite treats were marshmallows and cans of pie filling!

Denyse was happy for many years. When Denyse was about thirty, her "mom" died.

Everything changed with the death of Denyse's mom. Her "dad" was about eighty years old. He planned to sell his home. Then he would move away. He knew it would be hard for him to adjust to life without Denyse. He didn't want to give her away. But he knew he had to.

He had to find a home for Denyse. But where?

The perfect spot was in Florida. Denyse had the opportunity to move to an ape conservation center in Florida. She would be the oldest adult chimp at the center.

The center was founded in 1993. The center is a safe place for chimps and other apes. Many were once pets. Some were used for research. Some were circus performers.

There are thirty-six apes at the center. They live in large outdoor habitats. There are lots of swings and toys. There are also places to climb. The animals sleep in attached houses. They can rest in the houses at night. They can also nap in them during the day. The homes look like they are in a thick forest. There are many oak, pine, and fruit trees.

Apes are smart. The people at the center care for the apes. They make sure that they are not bored. They believe animals are mistreated when they do not have enough activities or exercise.

The animals eat different kinds of food. They drink fruit shakes. They also have activities everyday. They use boxes, brushes, shoes, and other toys.

People at the center try to entertain the animals too. Sometimes they blow bubbles to entertain them. The people also play musical instruments. The apes listen to guitars, flutes, and drums.

It took time for Denyse to adjust to her new home. She needed to follow the rules. She had to change her diet. Denyse started eating fresh leaves, fruits, vegetables, and other healthy treats.

Denyse met the other chimps at the center. But it took time. The people at the center were concerned for Denyse. They didn't want to scare her with too many changes. Now she lives with a small group of other chimps.

What Do You Think?

Why do you think Denyse might be afraid to meet other chimps?

In nature, many animals help each other out.

Helping Each Other

Grouper are lucky fish. When they need to be cleaned they simply open their mouths. Then other smaller fish go to work, eating tiny animals that can harm the grouper. The cleaning fish are lucky too. They get a free dinner! What a bargain!

If you were a bird would you fly into a crocodile's mouth? A bird called a plover (PLOH-ver) does this all the time! Nile crocodiles open their mouths wide. Birds fly in and clean their teeth. The plover get to eat the meat that they find. And the crocodiles are happy to have clean teeth.

Clownfish and sea anemones (uh-NEM-uh-neez) help each other out. Clownfish swim right above sea anemones. Other fish stay away because sea anemones can sting them. But clownfish have skin that protects them from stings. By staying near sea anemones, the clownfish are protected from large fish, and the clownfish help protect the sea anemones from butterfly fish. These fish like to eat sea anemones.

Honey badgers depend on honeyguide birds to lead them to beehives. The badgers open the hives. The hives are too hard for the birds to open on their own. After the badgers eat the honey, the birds eat the leftovers.

4 you 2 Do

Word Play

How many words can you make from the letters in this word? Make a list of five words that use at least three or four of the letters.

communicate

Making Connections

What types of things can we learn by studying animals such as Denyse?

On Paper

With a partner, write about how Dian Fossey or Denyse had to adjust in order to fit in.

Possible answers for Word Play: came, come, moment, mount, nice, once, fame, tone, tune, unit, unite

134

Glossary

ad·just (ə just´), *VERB.* to get used to: *Some wild animals never adjust to life in a zoo.* **ad·just·ed, ad·just·ing.**

a·dult (ə dult´ or ad´ ult), *NOUN.* a grown-up person: *An adult came with our group on our class trip.*

ad·ven·ture (ad ven´ chər), *NOUN.* an exciting experience: *Flying in an airplane for the first time is quite an adventure.*

at·tempt (ə tempt´), *NOUN.* a try; effort: *They made an attempt to climb the mountain.*

au·di·ence (o′ dē əns), NOUN. a group of people watching or listening to something: *The audience liked the circus.*

col·lec·tion (kə lek′ shən), NOUN. a group of things gathered from many places and belonging together: *Our library has a large collection of books.*

com·mu·ni·cate (kə myü′ nə kāt), VERB. to give or exchange information or news: *When my brother is away at school, I communicate with him by e-mail.* **com·mu·ni·cat·ed, com·mu·ni·cat·ing.**

de·light (di līt′), NOUN. great pleasure; joy: *The children took great delight in their toys.*

a in hat	ō in open	sh in she
ā in age	ȯ in all	th in thin
â in care	ô in order	ŦH in then
ä in far	oi in oil	zh in measure
e in let	ou in out	⌈ a in about
ē in equal	u in cup	e in taken
ėr in term	u̇ in put	ə = ⎨ i in pencil
i in it	ü in rule	o in lemon
ī in ice	ch in child	⌊ u in circus
o in hot	ng in long	

depth (depth), *NOUN.* the space from top to bottom: *The depth of the well is about twenty-five feet.*

dis·tance (dis´ təns), *NOUN.* the amount of space between things: *The distance from our house to school is two miles.*

fa·mous (fā´ məs), *ADJECTIVE.* very well known: *The famous singer was met by a large crowd at the airport.*

height (hīt), *NOUN.* how tall or high someone or something is: *The girl dove from a great height into the pool.*

im·pos·si·ble (im pos′ ə bəl), *ADJECTIVE.* not able to happen; *It is impossible to have an outdoor picnic when it is raining.*

in·stru·ment (in′ strə mənt), *NOUN.* something that makes music: *He can play the piano and two other instruments.*

in·ter·est (in′ tər ist),

1. *NOUN.* a feeling of wanting to know, see, do, own, or take part in something: *He has an interest in collecting stamps.* **in·ter·est·ed, in·ter·est·ing.**
2. *VERB.* to hold one's attention: *That kind of music does not interest me.* **in·ter·est·ed, in·ter·est·ing.**

mim·ic (mim′ ik), *VERB.* to copy closely; imitate: *A parrot can mimic voices.* **mim·icked, mim·ick·ing.**

a in hat	ō in open	sh in she
ā in age	ȯ in all	th in thin
â in care	ô in order	ᴛʜ in then
ä in far	oi in oil	zh in measure
e in let	ou in out	⎧ a in about
ē in equal	u in cup	⎪ e in taken
ėr in term	u̇ in put	ə = ⎨ i in pencil
i in it	ü in rule	⎪ o in lemon
ī in ice	ch in child	⎩ u in circus
o in hot	ng in long	

op·por·tu·ni·ty (op´ ər tu´ nə tē), *NOUN.* a good chance to do something: *I had an opportunity to earn some money.* PL. **op·por·tu·ni·ties.**

peak (pēk), *NOUN.* the pointed top of a mountain or hill: *We saw the snowy peaks in the distance.*

per·form (pər fôrm´), *VERB.* to act, play, sing, or do tricks in public: *The school band will perform at the assembly.* **per·formed, per·form·ing.**

po·si·tion (pə zish´ ən), *NOUN.* the place where a thing or person is: *The flowers grew in a sheltered position behind the house.*

rare (râr), *ADJECTIVE.* not often seen or found: *A house made from glass bottles is rare.*

re·al·ize (rē′ ə līz), *VERB.* to understand well: *Everyone realizes that she did a good job.* **re·al·ized, re·al·iz·ing.**

re·mark·a·ble (ri mär′ kə bəl), *ADJECTIVE.* worth noticing; extraordinary: *He has a remarkable memory for names and faces.*

a in hat	ō in open	sh in she
ā in age	ȯ in all	th in thin
â in care	ô in order	ŦH in then
ä in far	oi in oil	zh in measure
e in let	ou in out	ə = a in about
ē in equal	u in cup	e in taken
ėr in term	ů in put	i in pencil
i in it	ü in rule	o in lemon
ī in ice	ch in child	u in circus
o in hot	ng in long	

scale (skāl), *VERB.* to climb something: *He scaled the wall of ice using climbing tools.* **scaled, scal·ing.**

spe·cial (spesh´ əl), *ADJECTIVE.* different in a particular way: *Your birthday is a special day.*

sum·mit (sum´ it), *NOUN.* the highest point; top: *We climbed to the summit of the mountain.*

tal·ent (tal´ ənt), *NOUN.* a gift or ability for doing something: *She has a talent for music.*

u·nique (yü nēk), *ADJECTIVE.* very uncommon; being the only one of its kind: *His style of singing is unique.*

un·u·su·al (un yü´ zhü əl), *ADJECTIVE.* uncommon; not in common use: *The family went on an unusual trip.*

wa·ter·fall (wȯ´ tər fȯl´), *NOUN.* A stream of water that falls from a high place: *We went under a waterfall in Hawaii.*

a	in hat	ō	in open	sh	in she
ā	in age	ȯ	in all	th	in thin
â	in care	ô	in order	ŦH	in then
ä	in far	oi	in oil	zh	in measure
e	in let	ou	in out		a in about
ē	in equal	u	in cup		e in taken
ėr	in term	u̇	in put	ə=	i in pencil
i	in it	ü	in rule		o in lemon
ī	in ice	ch	in child		u in circus
o	in hot	ng	in long		

Acknowledgments

Illustrations

2, 6, 18–24 Stacey Schuett; **32, 46–52** Nicole Wong; **58–76** Julie Downing; **84, 96–102** Cathi Mingus; **120** Doug Knutson; **124–130** Doug Holgate.

Photographs

Every effort has been made to secure permission and provide appropriate credit for photographic material. The publisher deeply regrets any omission and pledges to correct errors called to its attention in subsequent editions.

Unless otherwise acknowledged, all photographs are the property of Pearson Education, Inc.

Photo locators denoted as follows: Top (T), Center (C), Bottom (B), Left (L), Right (R), Background (Bkgd)

Cover (TR) ©2006 Estate of Pablo Picasso/Artists Rights Society (ARS), New York/SCALA/Art Resource, NY, (CR) Dann Tardif/Corbis, (BL) Deborah Gilbert/Getty Images, (BR) Jeff Hunter/ Getty Images, (Back) Getty Images; **1** Richard T. Nowitz/Corbis; **2** (BR) Bill Curtsinger/National Geographic Image Collection; **3** (BR) ©Kim Taylor, (T) Getty Images, (TR) NASA/Corbis; **5** (C) Brand X Pictures/Getty Images, (C) GK & Vikki Hart/Getty Images; **6** (TR) ©Jeffrey L. Rotman/Corbis, (T) Brand X Pictures/Getty Images, (BR) Deborah Gilbert/ Getty Images; **8** (L) ©Jeffrey L. Rotman/Corbis, (TR) benn mitchell/Getty Images, (CR) John Giustina/ Getty Images; **9** Michelle Pedone/Getty Images; **10** Getty Images; **11** (T) Bettmann/Corbis, (B) The Kobal Collection; **12** (TL) Mike Theiller/Getty Images; **13** (BR) Karl Walter/Getty Images; **14** (BR) Leopold Mozart and His Two Children, Wolfgang Amadeus and Maria-Anna, Louis Carrogis Carmontelle (1717–1806)/British Libriary, UK/Bridgeman Art Library, (TL) Portrait of Wolfgang Amadeus Mozart (1756–91), Austrian composer, 1818, Barbara Kraft (1764–1825)/Gesellschaft der Musikfreunde, Wien, Austria/Bridgeman Art Library; **15** (TL) Icon SMI/ Corbis, (BR) Scott McDermott/Corbis; **16** (TL) Gary Bogdon/Corbis, (R) Gary Hershorn/Corbis; **17** (CR) ©2006 Estate of Pablo Picasso/Artists Rights Society (ARS), New York/SCALA/Art Resource, NY, (TR) Popperfoto/Alamy Images; **26** (C) Brad Hitz/Getty Images; **27** (TL) ©Michael St. Maur Sheil/Corbis, (CL, BC) Louis Wallach/Corbis; **28** (C) Deborah Gilbert/Getty Images, (TL) V & A Images/Victoria and Albert Museum; **29** (C) Getty Images, (T) Julia Smith/Getty Images; **31** (C) Mike Powell/Getty Images; **32** (BR) Zena Holloway/Getty Images; **33** (C) BananaStock; **34** (C) Jeff Vanuga/Corbis; **35** (T,) Getty Images; **36** (TR) David Trood/Getty Images; **38** (R) Mickey Cashew/Getty Images; **39** (L) Jimmy Chin/National Geographic Image Collection; **40** (BL) Johner/Johner Bildbyra AB, Sweden, (BR) Mura Dolphins/AFP?Getty Images/ NewsCom; **41** (L) Digital Vision/Thinkstock, (BR) Stockdisc; **42** (T) George Band/Alamy Images; **43** (B) Anne Keiser/National Geographic Image Collection; **44** (BR) ©Associated Press, (BL) Splash News/NewsCom; **45** (TL) Zigy Kaluzny/Stone/Getty Images; **54** (C, BL) Zena Holloway/Getty Images; **55** (C) Bill Curtsinger/National Geographic Image Collection; **56** (R) BananaStock; **57** (TR, TL, CR, BR, BL, Bkgd) Getty Images, (C) Mark Heithoff/Getty Images; **58** (TR) Getty Images, (BR) Gone Wild Limited/Getty Images, (TR) Karen Pearson/Getty Images; **59** (TL, T) Getty Images; **60** (CR) Karen Pearson/Getty Images, (L) Peter Beck/Corbis; **61** (BC) Ronnie Kaufman/Corbis, (TL) Tom Stewart/ Corbis; **63** (C) Ryan McVay/Thinkstock; **64** Getty Images; **68** (BR) Danny Lehman/Corbis; **78** (CL, BL) Getty Images, (BR) julie toy/Getty Images; **79** (TR) Blend Images/Getty Images, (TL, BR) Getty Images, (TL) Hiroshi Huguchi/Getty Images; **80** (BL) Getty Images, (TL) Gone Wild Limited/Getty Images, (BR) schnare & stief/Getty Images, (CR) Stockdisc; **81** (TR) Clarissa Leahy/Getty Images, (B) Dann Tardif/Corbis; **82** (TR, TL, BC) Getty Images; **83** (C) NASA/Corbis, (C) Original image courtesy of NASA/Corbis; **84** (TR) Francis G. Mayer/Corbis; **85** (L) Richard T. Nowitz/Corbis; **86** Underwood & Underwood/Corbis; **87** (R) Francis G. Mayer/ Corbis, (Bkgd) Getty Images, (TL) NASA, (BL) Wally McNamee/Corbis; **88** Roy Rainford/Getty Images; **90** (Bkgd) Hulton Archive/Getty Images, (R) M. H. Zahner/Corbis, (L) Niagara Falls Public Library; **92** ©Hulton Archive/Getty Images; **93** (T) Hulton Archive/Getty Images; **94** (C) Bettmann/Corbis; **104** (L) Igor Kvetko/Getty Images, (R) Jupiter Images; **105** (CR) Richard T. Nowitz/Corbis; **106** (T) Steve Boyle/Corbis; **107** (TR) Burke/Triolo Productions/ Jupiter Images; **109** (C) Blickwinkel/Alamy Images; **110** (TR) Time Life Pictures/Getty Images; **111** ©Royalty-Free/Corbis; **112** (C) ©Royalty-Free/ Corbis, (BL) Getty Images; **113** (TR) James Frank/ Alamy Images; **114** (BR) Adrian Sherratt/Alamy Images, (CL) Foodfolio/Alamy Images; **115** (TR) Big Cheese Photo; **116** (CL) Time Life Pictures/Getty Images; **117** (TC) Getty Images; **118** (BC) Yann Arthus/Corbis; **119** (CC) ©Royalty-Free/Corbis; **120** (BC) Yann Arthus/Corbis; **121** (C) Klaus Paysan/ Peter Arnold, Inc.; **122** (BC) Yann Arthus/Corbis; **123** (BR) Purestock; **132** (R) ©Kim Taylor, (L) Georgette Douwma/Getty Images; **133** (T) Jeff Hunter/Getty Images, (B) Martin Harvey/Corbis; **134** (TR) Corbis; **142** Digital Vision/Thinkstock.